Mexborough & Swinton

The Motor Buses

Stuart Emmett

Text © Stuart Emmett, 2023.
First published in the United Kingdom, 2023,
by Stenlake Publishing Ltd.,
54-58 Mill Square,
Catrine, Ayrshire,
KA5 6RD

Telephone: 01290 551122
www.stenlake.co.uk

ISBN 9781840339369

The publishers regret that they cannot supply copies of any pictures featured in this book.

References

- C. S. Dunbar, *Commercial Motor,* 27th April 1956, "About turn trolleybuses".
- *Buses Illustrated,* November to January 1962.
- Charles C Hall (1999) *Rotherham & District Transport, Volume 3, 1939 to 1984.*
- C. T. Goode, (1982) *The History of the Mexborough & Swinton Traction Company.*
- The PSV Circle/The Omnibus Society, *Yorkshire Traction Company Limited, Fleet History (1961 to 1984)*, PB21 Part 2.
- Joyce, King, Newman (1986) *British Trolleybus Systems.*

List of Abbreviations

BET: British Electric Transport
JOC: Joint Omnibus Company
M&S: Mexborough & Swinton Traction Company
NECC: National Electric Construction Company
OMO: one man operated
PAYE: pay as you enter
RCT: Rotherham Corporation Transport
YTC: Yorkshire Traction Company

Author's Note

I hope you enjoy the journey through this book which I have enjoyed researching and writing. The photographs came from various and many sources, and I am grateful to them for sharing their work and not keeping their images locked away.

It is not always possible to obtain perfect images of every bus operated. Those included in the book are used to present as complete a record as possible. If anyone can assist to fill in the gaps, then I will be delighted to hear from you.

The proceeds from the book sales, after deduction of costs, are going 100% to assist on bus preservation/archives. The author, as well as some of the image providers, have supplied their services free of charge to help this initiative.

Unless stated below, the pictures are from my own collection that is made up of our family pictures and other sources, some of which have proved impossible to locate; for these, I offer my apologies for the lack of accreditation.

Pictures/images are from the following people, and in no specific order: Roy Marshall, Peter Hirst, Craig Sheppard.

Also, from the following image providers: The Bus Archive, P.M. Photography, Mineralcraft, The Bus Gallery, Classic Bus Photos, Travel Lens Photographic.

Introduction

The main operating area of M&S was in a 6 miles square box north of Rotherham that contains Rawmarsh, Swinton, Mexborough and Conisbrough. Dissecting the box from bottom left to top right is the River Don that rises in the Pennines, west of Dunford Bridge, and flows for 70 miles eastwards, through Penistone, Sheffield, Rotherham. Mexborough, Conisbrough, Doncaster and Stainforth to join the River Ouse at Goole. The River Don parallels the road from Rotherham to Conisbrough. The road runs to the north of the river and for the most part between a quarter and one and a half miles from it.

In the 6 miles square box were many contrasts, with open green fields north of Rawmarsh at Warren Vale, industrial and colliery sites in Manvers Main, Denaby Main and elsewhere, narrow village type roads in Mexborough and Swinton, an ancient 12th century castle in Conisbrough and finally, the large steel works at Parkgate near Rawmarsh (that employed up to 10,000 people before its closure in 1985). In 1987 the site became, Parkgate Retail World and in 2018 the northern terminus for the Sheffield Supertram.

The former industrial base of the area created wide variations in bus headways, for example, one route had sixteen journeys before 0908 hours and then none until the last journey at 2253 hours. The M&S buses were literally driven to serve and connect the heavy industry in a relatively compact area. As a comparison of this compact area of large villages and small towns each with a population of between 15-20,000 people, the population of the compact M&S operating area, is just over half that of Rotherham with its 120,000 people.

The motor buses of M&S have received less attention than the single deck trolley bus fleet. This is perhaps not too surprising, but the motor bus fleet was interesting in itself and had developed from small fleets of single deckers providing feeders to the electric routes. Then in the mid 1950s single deckers were used to replace trolleybus and this cumulated in double deckers finally "seeing off" the trolleybuses in 1961. So, in the history of M&S, the main motor bus years were relatively short, lasting only from 1954 to 1969, when, 10 coaches, 9 single deckers and 21 double deckers were transferred into the larger Yorkshire Traction fleet.

Whilst the main M&S bus fleet were purchased new (and these were mainly standard BET group products), these were supplemented for short periods by double deckers from Southdown, a few running in their original livery.

Additionally, a small coach fleet provided excursions and undertook private hire work. Initially the coaches were bought new, and one at a time. However, from 1961, these were supplemented by other coaches bought from Yorkshire Traction, many from Southdown and the final three came from Northern General. The second-hand buys usually stayed for 2 to 3 years. For each of the 1966 and 1967 summer seasons, two coaches were also loaned from Southdown.

M&S15 was one of the first two double deckers to come from Southdown in October 1961 as the final Atlanteans (13/14) were going to be late delivered (they came in November 1962). 15 was a Leyland TD5 new in December 1938 with a 1950 Northern Counties body. The two were withdrawn in early 1963 and eventually scrapped by M&S. Roger Holmes

One of the ex-Southdown coaches was M&S 104 (LCD 859), one of three Leyland TS8 Beadle rebuilds with Beadle C35C bodies. They came to M&S in November/December 1962 and by November 1964 were scrapped. 104 is on hire to Yorkshire Traction and running here from Sheffield to Bridlington. *Roger Holmes*

History and date line

Whilst the full history of M&S has been well covered and some references are shown on page 2, the development of the motor bus and their routes ties into the overall company history, so an overview is provided below:

- 1905. Powers had earlier been obtained from Rotherham to Rawmarsh (Rycroft) and then quickly followed by a route from Rawmarsh to Old Toll Bar, near Denaby. The developer, however, went bankrupt so in stepped the National Electric Construction Company (NECC), who went onto finalise the system and provide the trams.

- 1907. A 7-mile route started from Rotherham to Denaby and went via Rawmarsh, Warren Vale, Woodman Inn, Swinton, Mexborough, and Old Toll Bar, near Denaby. In normal tramway style the depot was near the end of the route at Old Toll Bar. The operation started in February with an initial 20-minute headway from Rotherham to Rawmarsh and was then extended in August to Denaby. The headways changed to every 30 minutes, with shorts every 15 minutes from Swinton to Denaby and every 10 minutes from Rotherham to Parkgate. The route practically linked the Don Valley by tram via Rotherham to Sheffield and as it was the first route, it was later numbered route "A" by M&S (and 24 by Rotherham).

- 1908. From the 20th October the route was jointly run with Rotherham Corporation and changes were made by NECC to the trams' electrical input from contact studs in the track to, normal overhead wiring.

- 1910. Motor buses were tried and were hired in September from an associate company of NECC, delightfully named the Musselburgh & District Electric Light & Traction Company. Two routes were run from Mexborough, one over the tram route to Old Toll Bar, and the other from Mexborough via Manvers Main to Wath. However, objections came from Mexborough Council and in December 1910 the routes closed, with the buses leaving for pastures unknown.

- 1915. On 31st August, the first trackless/trolleybuses came; M&S were the first private company to operate trolleybuses in the country. Initially they extended the route just under 2 miles from the Old Toll Bar, Denaby to Conisbrough. This had a start/stop/start existence in the early years but was finally worked continuously from 1922 and when eventually linked back to Rotherham, became route "B" and Rotherham's 25.

- 1915. Meanwhile trolleybuses had also started from Mexborough to Manvers Main, but again with a start/stop existence until, finally running fully from 1921 (also reported as 1919). This was to eventually to become route "C". Near the Manvers Main terminus was a low bridge with a clearance of 13ft.1" (also reported as 12ft.9"). The area had its fair share of rail tracks with the Grand Central and Midland rail companies running virtually parallel from Rotherham to Swinton. This created the Manvers Main bridge and also additional bridges at Kilnhurst (10ft.9") and two at Swinton (near the Midland railway station at 13ft.9" and the Grand Central line towards Mexborough at 14ft.3"). The 13ft 9" bridge in Swinton was next to a bridge over the canal, creating a hump followed by a dive-under experience. More importantly for bus operations, however, was the level crossing at Denaby, as the frequent colliery rail traffic created a regular bottleneck.

From the pedestrian bridge, M&S 37 at Denaby Level Crossing on an all-clear day.

- So, by 1922 there were trams from Rotherham to Denaby, trolleybuses from Denaby to Conisbrough and also between Mexborough and Manvers Main; (a classic "T" shaped route system was now established with Rotherham to Mexborough forming the vertical part, and the horizontal having Manvers Main and Conisbrough)

- 1922 also brought the first new motor bus purchase of three Daimlers with Strachan and Brown bodies for a new 30-minute headway feeder service from Mexborough to Goldthorpe via Bolton on Dearne. The headway was soon reduced to every hour due to low usage and was passed over to Yorkshire Traction in 1929.

- 1925 and more buses (another Daimler and two Dennis) and another feeder service on 25th April, around 2 miles from Low Stubbin in Rawmarsh to Kilnhurst. This route survived. The buses were replaced in 1939 by an Albion from Hebble and 2 Leylands from Yorkshire Traction.

- 1927 saw another feeder service start on 10th June from Rawmarsh to Greasbrough. This also survived in various forms.

- 1928/1929 saw a rationalisation of the tram and trolleybus routes with the tram tracks nearing the end of their life; the last tram running from Rotherham to Mexborough in March 1929. By 10th March 1929 trolleybuses were supreme and were now running as follows:

    - Route "A", Rotherham to Mexborough and extended in January 1931 into a new housing estate at Adwick Road. (Joint with Rotherham).
    - Route "B", Rotherham to Conisbrough Low (Brook Square). (Joint with Rotherham).
    - Route "C", Manvers Main to Conanby/Conisbrough High.

Rotherham trolleybus at Conisbrough, Welfare Avenue Route C terminus. It is on an enthusiasts' tour as this location was not normally reached by Rotherham trolleybuses.

- 1929 saw a name change to the Mexborough & Swinton Traction Company (becoming a Limited company in 1953). In the same year, authority was given for motor buses to be used on the trolleybus routes.

- 1931. M&S became 100% owned by British Electric Transport (BET) and unlike many BET companies there was no part-owning or railway interests involved.

- 1933. To replace the older buses, two new Dennis single deck buses came, followed in 1935 by a 1928 Leyland from Yorkshire Traction. In turn these were replaced in 1939 by a 1928 Albion from Hebble, and two 1933 Leylands from Yorkshire Traction.

- 1934. A short trolleybus "run round" loop was opened on 15th October in Rawmarsh from Stocks Lane and Green Lane up to Rycroft on Kilnhurst Lane. This was to be the last trolleybus extension and the final position of the routes was as follows:

Final trolley bus routes

	From	To	Via
A	Rotherham	Mexborough (Adwick Road)	Parkgate, Rawmarsh, Woodman Inn, Swinton.
B	Rotherham	Conisbrough Low (Brook St.)	As above plus Mexborough, Denaby Main.
C	Manvers Main	Conanby/Conisbrough High (The Crescent)	Mexborough, Denaby Main.

Note:

- Rotherham routes were joint with Rotherham Corporation Transport.

- Manvers Main to Mexborough section stopped on 1st January 1961 and then ran for three months from Rotherham to Conanby/Conisbrough High until the whole system closed on 26th March 1961.

Coming down from Rawmarsh approaching Parkgate, 37 (JWW 375) heads for Rotherham followed by a Rotherham trolleybus. Sold to Bradford and rebodied there in 1962 (with sixth others) it became Bradford 845 and was the last one in public service on 26th March 1972.

- 1947. An extension was granted in May for a short spur from Adwick Road trolley terminus into the Windhill Estate. Whilst a long-desired extension, no capex could be found, so in came three new Bedford OBs and a second-hand Bedford OB from East Yorkshire. These replaced the earlier Hebble Albion, and the two YTC Leylands.

- The post-war trolleybuses in 1947 entered service in a green and cream livery, replacing the earlier red and brown colours.

- 1948. The Windhill Estate route opened on 1st December from Mexborough Railway Station and two more Bedford OBs were bought for early 1949 delivery.

- 1950. Two 1934 Leylands with 1939 Duple bodies came from YTC but left in late 1951. It was also announced in 1950 that there would be no more trolleybus extensions.

- 1951 Pay as you enter (PAYE) was introduced in April on the Windhill Estate route.

- 1951/1952, the four Bedfords went and were replaced by four 1939 AEC Regals from Devon General.

- 1953. The Windhill Estate route was closed on 30th June 1953, due to lack of use and it would be 1960 until it was served again. Therefore, the final two Bedfords left along with the four AEC Regals. An application was made in September for full motor bus operation. The days of trolleybuses were now numbered as six new Leyland single deckers were ordered, soon increased to ten to cover the four withdrawn Devon General Regals.

- 1954 saw the arrival of the ten new 44-seater single deckers. The first two were used on the 1953 route from Parkgate to Kilnhurst route (Route 5) and two on the 6th August on a revised route into the estates at Low Stubbin/Upper Hough and Monkwood from Rotherham (Route 6). The final six single deckers were used on the Rotherham to Rawmarsh Green Lane "short" route, when on 27th September, the short turn trolleybus route at Rawmarsh Green Lane from Rotherham was converted to motor bus operation. This was followed by the sale of six 1943 trolleybuses to nearby Doncaster Corporation Transport. The Weymann single deckers showed they were ideal for non-peak times, but had little room for standing at peak times. This was addressed in the subsequent order for new buses that created an extra internal space for standing passengers and was made possible by having single seats towards the front.

- 1955. In April a motor bus service, Route 4, ran from Rotherham, Parkgate, New Stubbin Colliery, Green Lane, Sandhill to Kilnhurst. Routes to Sandhill (Routes 4, 5) were designed to serve miners who were moving into the area, particularly from Scotland, and the National Coal Board built a new estate at Sandhill, known locally as "The Concrete Canyon". Additionally, two new and different motor buses joined, one a new Leyland/Burlingham Seagull coach for private hire work, the other a 1939 Leyland TS with ECW B35R body ex Maidstone & District. This stayed in service until 1959 when it was converted to a towing truck.

- 1955. Application was made for full day excursions up to 200 miles and half days around 90 miles. Initially a programme was offered to the East Coast resorts, like Whitby, Scarborough, and Bridlington along with country runs to the Peak District and the Yorkshire Dales.

- 1956. *Commercial Motor* reported that the passenger numbers over the year were 12.1 million on trolleybuses and 5.5 million for motor buses. As the vehicle annual mileages were about 1.2 million and 500,000 respectively, they concluded "that passengers average was about 10d a mile, which is fairly high". Additionally, they reported the "main line" from Rotherham to Rawmarsh had a service every 3 minutes.

- 1957. On 21st January the Highwoods estate at Mexborough was linked to the Ellershaw estate at Conisbrough (Route 1), and duplicated the trolleybus routes for much of the journey. On 2nd September, the Parkgate to Swinton Route 5, was extended at Swinton to the Cresswell Arms.

- 1957, three more single deckers came (numbered 50 to 52), this time with the so called "standee" bodies. These were amongst the first of this type in the BET group and had needed special authorisation; they also had a larger engine and a special front axle to cope with the extra front weight. With 32 or 34 seats and with room for 29 or 27 standing, the layout went through various changes from 1960, such as 37+25, 36+25 and were eventually changed to be 42+20 seaters with one becoming DP40F. Whilst receiving some criticism as "cattle trucks", the answer given was that passengers preferred to stand rather than wait on the pavement. There is no doubt that M&S thought such buses were successful.

- 1958. Another Leyland single decker came (the last of the standee type) and also another Leyland/Burlingham Seagull coach.

- 1959. Another Leyland single decker arrived, now with normal seating. The fleet balance reflected the operational changes made, with 19 trolleybuses and 16 single decker motor buses in service. In 1952 there had been 36 trolleybuses and just six single decker buses.

- 1960.The Windhill service was revived on 22nd February running via Adwick Road and then into Mexborough and also Swinton, before turning round at either Cresswell Arms or Brookside on the road to Kilnhurst (Route 3). Four more Leyland single deckers came. Late in the year came many new Leyland Atlanteans for trolleybus replacement, these being stored pending events in March 1961.

One of the trolleybus-replacing Atlanteans seen in Rotherham. Roger Holmes

- 1961. The main event was the cessation on 1st January of the trolleybus Manvers Main to Conisbrough High route, and after Mexborough, it then ran to Rotherham until 26th March. Then, the other two trolleybus routes finished, (these being those joint with Rotherham CT from Rotherham to Mexborough Adwick Road and to Conisbrough Low). Eleven new Leyland Atlantean double deckers entered service and introduced integrated headways and joint services with Rotherham covering all the main four terminals at Rotherham and Manvers Main/Highwood with those at Conisbrough High/Ellershaw Estate and Conisbrough Low/Windmill Estate. The change was reported to offer increased seat availability as follows:

  ✓ Rotherham to Conisbrough Low. With the Atlanteans on a 12-minute headway, there now were 265 seats per hour, against 192 with trolleybuses.

  ✓ Rotherham to Rawmarsh Green Lane at peak with 44-seater single deckers on an 8-minute headway, now 330 seats per hour, against 256 for the trolleybuses.

Sunday 26th March 1961 with the trolleybus procession that ran from Old Toll Bar to Rotherham, where the official party changed buses and went to Sheffield to commemorate the last BET (British Electric Traction) electric operation, led by former 29 (FWX 913) that had been cut down and carried the Rawmarsh Brass Band. The chassis went to Bradford and was rebodied to become Bradford's 843 (in a batch of seven, their last trolleybuses). Then on Friday 24th March 1972, 843 became the last trolleybus used on a scheduled service in the UK.

- The motor buses received after 1961 will be covered fully in the forthcoming "Fleet" section and in the final decade of M&S, many interesting buses entered service, including many second-hand purchases.

- 1965. On 8th February an express limited stop OMO service from Windhill in Mexborough to Sheffield started running jointly with Rotherham Corporation Transport and Sheffield Joint Omnibus Committee, though only 'on paper' and not in practice. This route was in response to one granted to the independent Dearnways of Goldthorpe.

- 1966. In May 1966 Mexborough applied for permission to operate a service using the new M1 motorway into Leeds. Despite advertising the service as commencing from February 1965(!) it was joint with Rotherham and Sheffield Joint Omnibus Committee. It seems that optimism had not been translated into practicalities as it met serious opposition from YTC, Burrows, West Riding, Sheffield JC, and Rotherham CT, along with British Rail. The May 1966 meeting was adjourned and it was not until 30th April 1968 that the application was heard, when approval was given for routes from Sheffield to Halifax, Bradford, and Leeds. However later, after M&S was moved into YTC on 1st October 1969, six services started on 18th October using the M1 northbound (these included the X35 and X36 from Mexborough). Named "the White Rose Express" this consortium had initially seven operators, Hebble, West Riding, YTC, Yorkshire Woollen, Sheffield, Rotherham, and Bradford. The services were interworked with six coaches and with an additional one for the Mexborough routes that bypassed Sheffield, but these express services are another story!

- In 1966 on repaints, the fleet name was changed from being shown in full as "Mexborough & Swinton" to now show, "Mexborough".

- 1967. In April with YTC and Rotherham CT, a service was started from Rotherham to West Melton via Wath (route 28) and this later interworked with the Conisbrough service. Additionally, in 1967, some management functions of M&S were taken on by YTC.

- 1968. The Old Toll Bar depot was closed.

- 1969. The National Bus Company was formed and locally this meant M&S now had a common owner with YTC. No surprises then that in October 1969 M&S were placed into Yorkshire Traction, along with the Dale Road depot and 40 buses. Three single deckers ordered by M&S arrived in May 1970 and went straight into the YTC fleet.

- One of the most profitable companies in the former BET structure was no more.

THE 628 to 630H were ordered by M&S for the "White Rose Express" Sheffield to Leeds consortium. They were Daimler SRG6LX with Marshall DP45F bodies and the last one is seen here off a X35 from Leeds, one of the routes they were ordered for. The two "White Rose" Mexborough routes were to be withdrawn in May 1975 and the X36 now ran three times a day from Rotherham, operated by the recently formed South Yorkshire PTE.

Motor Bus Routes

The original trolleybus routes after the initial incremental tram conversions were relatively static. The motor bus routes were by comparison "chopped/changed" in response to the building of new housing estates and the linking of routes to achieve operational efficiencies. Accordingly, these routes are shown in the following three tables, the first covering the early situation, the next in 1961 with the revised motor bus routes after the conversion from trolleybuses, and the last one from May 1969 that uses the "last" M&S timetable before their absorption into Yorkshire Traction.

Early motor bus routes

From	To	Via	Origins or Comments
Mexborough	Wath	Manvers Main	1910 start and finish
Mexborough	Old Toll Bar, Denaby		1910 start and finish
Mexborough	Goldthorpe	Bolton on Dearne	1922 to 1929 passed to YTC
Low Stubbin	Kilnhurst	Rawmarsh	1925 and into Route 6
Rawmarsh	Greasborough		1927 and into Route 5
Mexborough	Windhill Estate		1948 to 1953 and into Route 3 in 1960

1961 Motor Bus routes

n.	From	To	Via	Origins and/or Comments
1	Manvers Main or Highwoods.	Conanby/Conisbrough (High) or Ellershaw Estate.	Mexborough. Denaby.	21st January 1957 from Highwoods. Ex TB "C" from 2nd January 61. *
3	Brookside near Swinton or Cresswell Arms, Swinton.	Windhill Crescent near Mexborough.	Mexborough Adwick Road.	Started in 1960 and was part of the former 1948 to 1953 Windhill route.
4	Rotherham	Kilnhurst	New Stubbin Colliery, Rawmarsh Green Lane, Sandhill Estate.	Started 1955
5	Parkgate or New Stubbin	Swinton Cresswell Arms (on Bow Broom Estate).	Rawmarsh, Sandhill, Kilnhurst, Brookside.	10th June 1927 Greasborough to Rawmarsh.
				22nd February 1953. Parkgate to Kilnhurst.
				August 1954. Kilnhurst to Woodman Inn.
				Former "R" route from Greasborough to Woodman Inn.
6	Rotherham	Upper Haugh (near to Low Stubbin.	Monkwood Rawmarsh (Stocks Lane)	25th April 1925 Low Stubbin, Monkwood, Rawmarsh to Kilnhust.
				"M" route before 1955, Rotherham to Monkwood.
6A	Rotherham	Thorogate	Rawmarsh	The 6A ran alternate to route 6 (at peak 30 mins for 6 and 6A in 1960).
7	Rotherham	Rycroft	Rawmarsh (Green Lane).	Former "K". Rotherham to Kilnhurst Road at Rycroft.
7A	Rotherham	Rycroft	Rawmarsh (Green Lane). Sandhill Estate.	Former "S". Rotherham to Sandhill Estate and Rycroft.

n.	From	To	Via	Origins and/or Comments
8	Rotherham	Mexborough Adwick Road	Rawmarsh, Woodman Inn. Swinton. Mexborough.	Ex TB "B" from 26th March 61. *
9	Rotherham	Conisbrough Low- Windmill Estate	Rawmarsh, Woodman Inn. Swinton. Mexborough. Denaby.	Ex TB "A" from 26th March 61. *
9A	Rotherham	Conisbrough High- Ellershaw Estate	Rawmarsh, Woodman Inn. Swinton. Mexborough. Denaby. Conisbrough Low.	Former Bus route "W". Ex TB "A" from 26th March 61. *

Notes:

*Routes 1, 8, 9, 9A had integrated headways and joined Rotherham and Manvers Main to Mexborough, Conanby/Conisbrough High and Low.

- Origins are the routes "foundation" (with some possible overlap in developments between routes 4 to 6).
- 1 to 6 were single decked with 7 to 9 double decked.
- Route letters were replaced by numbers after the trolleybuses finished.

1969 Final Bus Routes

n.	From	To	Via	M-Sat Headway	JT	Comments
1	Manvers Main. (11 trips only, most from Mexborough Drill Hall)	Conisbrough High, Ellershaw Estate.	Highwoods, Mexborough, Denaby.	20 mins	26 min	
4	Rotherham	Manor Farm Estate via Greasborough or via Rawmarsh.	Parkgate, then: Nether Haugh; Monkwood. Upper Haugh.	60 mins 60 mins	21 min 20 min	
5	Rotherham	Conisbrough Low, Windmill Estate.	Parkgate, Rawmarsh, Kilnhurst, Swinton Cresswell, Mexborough. Adwick, Windhill, Denaby, Conisbrough Low, Brook Square.	60 mins	*	Joint with RCT.
5	Parkgate	Cresswell Arms Swinton	Rawmarsh, Sandhill Estate, Brookside.	Sunday pm only 9 tips	25 min	Joint with RCT.
5a	Rawmarsh	Swinton	Kilnhurst	**	**	Colliery trips
6	Rotherham	Rawmarsh Circular	Thorogate and Main Street Rawmarsh.	20 mins	33 min ***	Joint with RCT.
7	Rotherham	Rawmarsh Circular	Main Street Rawmarsh and Thorogate.	20 mins	33 min ***	Joint with RCT.
8	Rotherham	Mexborough Highwoods Hotel	Rawmarsh, Woodman Inn, Swinton, Adwick Road.	20 mins	29 min	Joint with RCT.

n.	From	To	Via	M-Sat Headway	JT	Comments
9	Rotherham	Conisbrough Windmill Estate	Rawmarsh, Woodman Inn, Swinton, Denaby, Conisbrough Low.	20 mins	40 min	Joint with RCT.
28	Rotherham	West Melton or extended to Brampton ****	Rawmarsh, Woodman Inn, Wath.	60 mins ****	28 min	Joint with YTC & RCT ****
90	Mexbrorough Windhill	Sheffield	Swinton, Rawmarsh. Rotherham	60 mins	48 min	Joint with RCT and Sheffield JOC. Limited Stop.

Notes:

- Headways can vary during the day. The one shown is the main one used.
- JT = journey time for a one-way trips.
- 4 to 5A and 90 are OMO, started in 1961.

* Route 5 Monday to Saturday journey trip times are 66 mins out and, a 24 mins circular at Conisbrough, plus 68 mins back, so the round-trip JT is 158 mins. This is a joined-up series of former "local" routes and clearly not intended for through passengers.

** Route 5A. On Monday to Friday this was a series of trips to/from Kilnhurst and New Stubbin collieries, with six morning and ten afternoon/evening journeys, and journey times ranging from 14 mins to 60 mins. On Saturday there were just four trips with journey times between 8 and 22 mins.

*** Route 6 & 7 are round trip times

**** Route 28 Up to 1030 and from 1900, Route 28 ran every 30 mins, mainly to West Melton only. After 1030 to 1800 the hourly service was limited stop and continued for 5 mins to Brampton, with no change to journey times. There was also before 1030, one limited stop inbound journey and one return journey.

Fleet in Pictures

These are ordered by the year into service and divided into single stage deckers, coaches and double deckers. Please note that the fleet numbers, were not always used in chronological order, and also some fleet numbers were re-used.

The single decker stage buses

78 (GWU 856) was one the three new Bedford OBs bought new and entered service in February 1948 numbered 77 to 79. With Duple Vista C29F bodies, they finished up in June 1952 with Sheffield United Tours, Sheffield but did not stay long before being sold to dealer, Cowley who handled many withdrawn buses from BET companies. From Cowley they passed in 1953 to independent operators based in Northamptonshire, London, and West Wales.

Another Bedford OB accompanied these three OBs, 80 (EBT 240) with a Roe B32F body new in September 1946 to an operator in Hunmanby, East Yorkshire and taken on in November 1947 by East Yorkshire MS who did not use it. M&S received EBT 240 in January 1948 where it lasted until 1952 when the engine failed. Used and repaired by a local Conisbrough company, it then went in 1958 to Wye Valley Motors in Hereford. R Marshall

81 (HWU 479) was one of two new in February 1949. 81/82 were Bedford OBs but with Duple Mark IV B30F bodies. These were the last OBs to leave when in 1953 they passed to dealers, Cowley in Salford. R Marshall

83 (AWA 331) with sister 84 were two 1934 Leyland LT5A, new to Hancock in Sheffield but now with 1939 Duple bodies that came in December 1949 from SUT. Entering service in May 1950, they left the following year. Former 83 is seen as a mobile shop. No in-service picture was found. Craig Sheppard collection

The four 1948 Bedford OBs were replaced in May and July 1952 by four 1939 AEC Regals from Devon General numbered 85 to 88 (DDV 447, 441, 442, 451) and had Harrington B35F bodies, rebuilt by Portsmouth Aviation in 1948. After two years they were sold on to the dealers, Cowley in 1954. The third one, 87 (DDV 442) is seen above, with its front wheel chocked at Dale Road depot. R Marshall

In 1954 ten Leyland PSUC1/1 with Weymann B44F bodies were delivered (four in March, two in April, two in July and two in August) registered MWU 140 to 149. They were in the almost overall green livery in the trolleybus style, but without a cream front "V". 41 was one of the first received and the batch survived until October 1967 when they all went to Cowley in Salford. Four went for scrap and six to McAlpine with some used as site huts. *PM Photography*

41 looking shiny new after a repaint. R. Marshall

The batch later received this more cream livery as shown on 45 that has also received a two-vent grill at the lower front. One of the ex-Southdown double deckers is following in the distance. PM Photography

40 now has the changed lower front grill, along with a cream livery that was also applied to 49 to show they were dual purpose buses after receiving high back seats and reclassified to be DP44F. The seats were retained on withdrawal.

Dual purpose 49 shows better the extended wheel green flashing that it and 40 had. Roy Marshall

A rather strange purchase in May 1955 was the FKO 81, a 1939 Leyland TS8 with ECW B35R body. Numbered 90 it came from the green livered Maidstone & District fleet. Withdrawn in 1959 it became a towing wagon. Roy Marshall

The former 90 in its new towing wagon role from September 1959 until 1966. It was initially painted red, I am told to use up the paint used in the pre-1947 livery. PM Photography

In January and October 1957 came 50 to 52, three more Leyland/Weymanns registered SWW 50/51 and TWY 52. The external body was slightly changed from the earlier batch having a larger windscreen with a nearside opening window and no front lower vents. Internally though the bodies were quite different, being the first of the "standee" layout that was described earlier in the timeline for 1957. All three were transferred to YTC in October 1969. Roy Marshall

52 with Conisbrough Castle in the background, the oldest standing structure in South Yorkshire and in the care of English Heritage. Travel Lens Photographic

The external differences between the first and later Weymann single deckers can be compared, with 40 & 52 comparison. The "standee" experiment finished in the late 1960s when the buses changed back to the B42F, 52 being converted to DP40F in October 1967 then painted in the more cream livery but with an extra lower green band.

56 now has larger lower front vents. 53 (UWY 53) was another new single decker and originally standee fitted in July 1958. However, the subsequent ones were not, these being 54 (WWW 54) in February 1959, and 55 to 58 (YWT 55 to 58) in February 1960. 55 to 58 were the last M&S new stage bus single deckers. All were to pass to YTC in October 1969.

Coach Fleet

100 was new in May 1955 and was the first new coach, a Leyland PSUC1/2 with Burlingham Seagull IV body C41F body and with the front indicator option, allegedly originally sponsored by Ribble. 100 eventually went to YTC in October 1969, but before then it had a rebuild. PM Photography

100 after its extensive rebuild in July 1968. Most of the below window trim and lower body panelling was replaced, and a flat glass windscreen and PAYE equipment were fitted. Roy Marshall

101 was another Leyland, new in May 1958 in time for the summer season. With a Burlingham Seagull VI body with flat windscreen glass, it was fitted for PAYE work in September 1968 and in October 1969 went over to YTC.

102 (XWX 376) was a Ford 570E with Plaxton Consort IV C41F body. New in 1959 to Camplejohn Bros in Darfield, it passed to YTC in January 1961 who passed it straight to M&S. Withdrawn in 1968 it initially, via the dealers Norths, worked for Boddy in Bridlington from 1968 to 1971. PM Photography

LCD 856, 859 to 860 were numbered 103 to 105 with M&S. New to Southdown in May 1952, they were Leyland TS8 Beadle rebuilds with Beadle C35C bodies and came to M&S in November/December 1962. By November 1964 they were scrapped by M&S. In the rear is another former Southdown bus (FCD 511), which had a roof gantry fitted for depot roof repairs. *Peter Hirst*

An offside view of 104. R. Marshall

In December 1963 came two all-Leylands from Southdown 106/107 (LUF 621 and 637) new in 1952. These were followed in November 1964 by two others, 104/105 (LUF 639/640) that replaced the Beadles 103 to 105. In 1967, 106/107 and 105 were sold to dealers Cowley. 104 was converted in November 1966 to a breakdown tender to replace 90. PM Photography

104 after its conversion. It made the YTC transfer in October 1969. PM Photography

108 (EWW 108C) was the first of three Leyland PSU3/3R with Duple Northern C49F bodies. 108 was new in April 1965 and went over to YTC in 1969 as did the other two, 109 (KWW 109D) new in January 1966 and 110 (NWW 110E) new in March 1967. To assist the coach fleet, in summer 1966 and 1967, two coaches were loaned from Southdown each year. In 1966 came VUF 930/931 Commer Avenger IVs with Burlingham C35C bodies new in 1959. In 1967 the two were OUF 100/108 Leyland PSUC1/1 with Beadle C41C bodies new in 1955. Roy Marshall

103 (OUF 834) was another buy from Southdown in November 1965, a 1955 Leyland PSU1/11 (7'6" wide) with a rare Harrington Wayfarer C26C body. It stayed with M&S until November 1968 and went to a builder in York. PM Photography

112 to 114 (PCN 2 to 4) came from Northern in October 1967 when they replaced 105 to 107, the all-Leylands from Southdown. 1963 Bedford SB5 with Harrington C41F bodies, they came instead of the initially planned, four similar, coaches from Trent. **The Bus Gallery**

In March 1968 from the dealers, Yeates, came two Bedfords. Although numbered in the coach series, they were also used on "quiet" bus routes and seem to have replaced 102 (XWX 376) and 103 (OUF 834) in the coach fleet. On the right is Bedford 115 (539 DWT) with Yeates DP44F body new in April 1963 to Store (Reliance) of Stainforth, near Doncaster. Like its following half twin, it went over to YTC in October 1969. Roy Marshall

116 (TDO 294) was a Bedford SB1 with Yeates DP41F body new in September 1961 to Camplin and Sons, of Donnington. The two Bedfords (115/116) were quickly sold by YTC to Baddeley Brothers in Holmfirth in December 1969. Roy Marshall

Double Decker Fleet

1960 brought the first Atlanteans that entered service in March 1961 after the trolleybuses finished. Numbered 1 to 11 (7001 to 7011 WU) with Weymann L72F bodies all passed to YTC in 1969. 1 is seen in Rotherham Bus Station with 52 behind and in its second livery version with upper front and rear extra cream. This seems possibly to highlight the advertising. **Classic Bus**

9 approaches a lady holding out her hand at Parkgate.
Classic Bus

9 showing the lower front "Maidstone & District" style that was said by some to follow the trolleybus "V" shape. Bus Gallery

12 (6812 WX) quickly followed the first eleven in July 1961. Seen at Parkgate by the former steelworks. Peter Hirst

The final two Atlanteans (13/14) were going to be late delivered, soauthorisation was given to buy 15/16 (FCD509/511) from Southdown. These entered service with M&S in October 1961. 15 is seen here outside Dale Road Depot on a driver changeover. Leyland TD5s new in December 1938 and January 1939 with Northern Counties bodies from 1950, they were withdrawn in early 1963 and scrapped by M&S. PM Photography

16 is "smoking" towards Mexborough and, like 15, retained the Southdown livery. One of only two that kept the livery, with other Southdowns repainted either by M&S or by fellow BET company Trent in Nottingham.

The last two "standard" Atlanteans came in November 1962 numbered 13/14 (8413-8414 YG. 14 is seen during construction work at Rotherham Bus Station on the April 1967-started route, joint with YTC and Rotherham CT, from Rotherham to West Melton via Wath (route 28). This was soon to be interworked with the Conisbrough Route 9. Roy Marshall

M&S seems again to have found itself short of double deckers as in April and May 1963 came four former Southdown buses. Two replaced the earlier 15/16 Leyland TDs. They were numbered 15 to 18 (GUF 667/9/71/82), however 17 was not operated. They were early post-war Leyland PD1s, new in 1946 with almost utility style Park Royal bodies and ran with M&S until 1965/1966, when like 17 before them in 1963, they were scrapped. 18 is seen here still in service with the "old" 16 behind in a state of canalisation and alongside a snowplough parked up awaiting winter. *Roy Marshall*

Leyland PD 18 heads for Rotherham.
PM Photography

After 1962 the double deckers of choice were Daimler Fleetlines. The first one seen here in Rawmarsh was ordered in July 1963 and entered service in September 1964 as 19 (CWY 319B). Roger Holmes.

In November 1964, joining the GUF registered buses numbered 15, 16 and 18, were two Southdown JCDs. The Park Royal GUFs had a curved rear and an unusual lower deck window.

Above: In November 1964, came two more Southdown buses. 1948 Leyland PD2/1 with Leyland H54R bodies and numbered 17 and 20 (numbers 18 and 19 being in use) and registered JCD 29 and 39. At Parkgate, with 17 heading for Conisbrough with the rear of 20 heading in the other direction. PM Photography

Left: 20 had this unusual front destination "box" that had been modified by Southdown to take a three-digit route number mainly used on Worthing locals. It became a learner bus in December 1967 and passed to YTC in October 1969, whilst sister 17 was sold to Norths, dealers in June 1966 who sold it on locally in Goldthorpe, where it was scrapped.

The final ex-Southdown double deckers arrived in October/November 1965 and stayed until autumn 1968. They replaced 15, 16 and 18 and were numbered 21 to 24, although 21 was renumbered 25 in December 1967 with the delivery of new Fleetline 21. All Leyland PD2/12s with H58RD bodies and registered KUF 704/707/722/723. New in 1951, 22 saw further service with a cleaning company in Leeds, 24 went to Holland and 25 (ex 21) and 23 were sold for scrap. PM Photography

24 rests in the depot and behind is one of the Weymann single deckers showing the rear route number box. PM Photography

Coming just after the ten Weymann single deckers 40 to 49 had been withdrawn in October 1967, was a batch of six of Fleetlines. These had a new body maker for M&S, Northern Counties. Rather strangely numbered around the 1964 Fleetline 19, they were numbered 15 to 18 and 20/21, registered RWY 515-518F and 520/521F. 17 is seen here with an unusual top 60% pennant style destination blind. The choice of a white/cream roof was perhaps copying the Southdown livery style? In 1969, towards the end of M&S, 15 to 18 went to West Riding, Wakefield and 20/21 went to YTC in October 1969. **Peter Hirst**

23 was one of the four final deliveries to M&S in October 1968 and is leaving Rotherham Bus Station with a Rotherham single decker alongside. The batch was 22 to 25 (WWU 922-925G) and retained the Northern Counties bodywork as well as the normal M&S green roofed double decker livery. They had replaced 21 to 24, the former Southdown Leyland KUFs. 22 to 25 went across to YTC in October 1969. **The Bus Gallery**

Towards the end of M&S in 1969 various vehicles came on hire from YTC, including three Leyland single deckers (EHE 939, 948 and WHE 213). Three double deckers also came and were further Fleetlines new in to YTC in 1968 with NCME bodies registered NHE 40 to 42F (from the batch 40 to 46F). NHE 40F is seen above in Rotherham on M&S route 7 with a "home" M&S, 8413 YG, behind.

The story behind this loan was more complicated, however, as at the time West Riding had recently been bought by NBC, who in 1969 started to replace the large fleet of Guy Wulfrunians with Bristol Lodekkas from many NBC fleets. As part of this programme, four Leyland Atlanteans with Willowbrook bodies already built and painted in Devon General livery but not yet delivered, were due to be sent to West Riding, but instead came to YTC who registered them RHE 447 to 450G and ran for a few years in the Devon General livery. West Riding then in turn, got the ex-M&S Fleetlines RWY 515 to 518F, as mentioned above. Craig Sheppard collection